Kobe Bryant

SUPERSTARS IN THE WORLD OF BASKETBALL

Mason Crest
450 Parkway Drive, Suite D
Broomall, PA 19008
www.masoncrest.com

Printed and bound in the United States of America.

First printing
9 8 7 6 5 4 3 2 1

Series ISBN: 978-1-4222-3101-2
ISBN: 978-1-4222-3108-1
ebook ISBN: 978-1-4222-8798-9

The Library of Congress has cataloged the
hardcopy format(s) as follows:
    Library of Congress Cataloging-in-Publication Data

Indovino, Shaina Carmel.
  Kobe Bryant / Shaina Indovino.
    pages cm. — (Superstars in the world of basketball)
  ISBN 978-1-4222-3108-1 (hardback) — ISBN 978-1-4222-3101-2 (series) — ISBN 978-1-4222-8798-9 (ebook) 1. Bryant, Kobe, 1978—Juvenile literature. 2. Basketball players—United States--Biography—Juvenile literature. I. Title.
  GV884.B794I53 2014
  796.323092—dc23
  [B]
                                        2014007852

Contents

KEY ICONS TO LOOK FOR:

Text-Dependent Questions: These questions send the reader back to the text for more careful attention to the evidence presented there.

Words to Understand: These words with their easy-to-understand definitions will increase the reader's understanding of the text, while building vocabulary skills.

Series Glossary of Key Terms: This back-of-the book glossary contains terminology used throughout this series. Words found here increase the reader's ability to read and comprehend higher-level books and articles in this field.

Research Projects: Readers are pointed toward areas of further inquiry connected to each chapter. Suggestions are provided for projects that encourage deeper research and analysis.

Sidebars: This boxed material within the main text allows readers to build knowledge, gain insights, explore possibilities, and broaden their perspectives by weaving together additional information to provide realistic and holistic perspectives.

Words to Understand

professional: Paid to play (usually in a league like the NBA).
varsity: The highest-level team that represents a high school or college.

Coached by His Father

Kobe Bryant and his teammates are standing on a podium in the center of the Olympic Stadium. Beside them are members of the Russian and Chinese basketball teams. They have come from miles away for a chance to earn the Olympic gold medal. All three teams have fought hard to get to this point, and it really shows.

Thousands of fans in the crowd cheer loudly as medals for each member of the three teams are brought out on trays. The Russian team is given the bronze, and the Spanish team is given the silver. That leaves the United States, which has earned the gold. Kobe and his teammates are tired and sweaty, but they are also smiling. Over the past few weeks, the U.S. team won eight games and gone undefeated to claim the title of Olympic champions.

Music plays in the background as the crowd cheers loudly. The audience claps and cheers as gold medals are given to each member of the U.S. team. As each team member receives his medal, the player's name is called. When Kobe Bryant's name is announced, the crowd goes wild. He waves to his fans and smiles as the heavy medal is placed around his neck. Moments like this make basketball worth playing.

Kobe dunks the ball during a game against China during the 2008 Beijing Olympic Games.

For many athletes, competing in the Olympic Games is the highlight of their careers. The athletes chosen to compete for each country are the best in the world. Kobe Bryant joined the USA basketball team twice and helped win a gold medal both times. The first time was in 2008. The second time was just four years later, in 2012. Winning an international championship is never easy. Every member of the U.S. basketball team needed to give their all to snag the gold.

After winning his second Olympic gold medal, Kobe announced he would not return to the Olympics. "This is it for me. The other guys are good to go," he said. Kobe believes his other teammates are strong enough to win the next world championship without him. In 2016 the world will know if he is correct.

As of 2013, Kobe has been playing in the NBA for over fifteen years. He started his NBA career right out of high school, but that's not when Kobe's love for the game began. He's been playing since he was just three years old! Through hard work and determination, he has risen to the top. Now he's one of the greatest basketball players in the history of the sport!

When Kobe was growing up, his favorite basketball player was Magic Johnson, who played for the Los Angeles Lakers. As a Laker, Magic Johnson became an NBA champion five times. Kobe looked up to Magic Johnson, and the Lakers became Kobe's favorite team. One day, Kobe hoped to play for that team, too. And he did!

Kobe dreamed of being a famous basketball player from the moment he could dribble a ball. Today he has a long list of accomplishments. He has won international titles, been part of an NBA championship team five times, and was the NBA's Most Valuable Player (MVP) of 2008.

SPORTS IN THE FAMILY

Kobe Bean Bryant was born on August 23, 1978, in Philadelphia, Pennsylvania. He has two older sisters, Shaya and Sharia. Growing up, all three children were athletic and liked

The Beijing basketball stadium where the basketball games of the 2008 Olympics were held.

The Wells Fargo center, where the Philadelphia 76ers play. Kobe's dad played for the 76ers during his time in the NBA. Later, Kobe would train with the team.

Kobe loved sports at an early age. Living in Italy, Kobe loved both soccer and basketball. But in the end, Kobe followed his father into basketball.

to play sports. One of the reasons Kobe and his sisters were so athletic is because of their father. Joe "Jellybean" Bryant is a former NBA player. He played for the Philadelphia 76ers, the San Diego Clippers, and the Houston Rockets during his time in the NBA.

Like many sons, Kobe wanted to follow in his father's footsteps. He went with his dad to practice and even watched him play at official games. Kobe watched his father on television and practiced with his own plastic ball and hoop. He pretended to be his dad, shooting his tiny basketball at the same time his father did on television. By Kobe's third birthday, his mind was made up. He was going to become an NBA star—just like his father—and no one was going to stop him.

When Kobe was six years old, his father decided to stop playing in the NBA. The family moved to Italy, so Joe could play basketball in an Italian league. Adjusting to life in a foreign country was difficult at first. Luckily, Kobe had his family to help him get used to it. Kobe and his sisters learned to speak Italian while they lived there. Kobe is still fluent in Italian.

While living in Italy, Kobe learned how to play soccer. Soccer is a very popular sport, especially in Europe. Kobe played both basketball and soccer while he lived in Italy. Kobe was very good at both sports. He has said he might have become a *professional* soccer player if he stayed in Italy. But even though Kobe liked to play soccer, his favorite sport was still basketball.

Growing up with a basketball player as a dad meant Kobe had many opportunities most kids don't usually get. Kobe learned a lot about basketball from his father before he even started playing on a team. His father also made a lot of money as a basketball player. He could afford to pay for his children to get a good education and travel all over the world. And when they lived in Italy, Joe Bryant sent Kobe back to the United States to play in a summer basketball league. Kobe improved his skills and studied the NBA while he was visiting.

Because satellite television wasn't around yet, and the Internet wasn't widely used, Kobe couldn't watch live NBA games while he lived in Italy in the 1980s. Kobe's grandparents knew how important basketball was to him and found a way to help him. They lived in the United States and recorded the NBA games for Kobe. Each week, they sent videotapes of the games to Italy for Kobe to watch. That way, Kobe could keep up with American basketball. Kobe's father watched the tapes with his son and used them to give him pointers on how to be a better basketball player. By understanding what was happening during a professional game, Kobe was able improve his game.

RETURNING TO THE UNITED STATES

In 1991 the Bryants moved again. This time they went to France. Joe finished the 1991–1992 basketball season and then retired. He quit for a few reasons, but the most important was his family. His daughters were ready to go to college, and Kobe was about to enter high school. They needed a more stable life and couldn't be moving around as much. Joe was also getting older, and playing basketball put a lot of stress on his body. He was almost forty and his body couldn't handle it anymore.

Text-Dependent Questions

1. How many medals did Kobe win at the 2008 Olympic Games? Will he be competing in the Olympics again?
2. What teams did Joe Bryant play for in the NBA?
3. How did Joe Bryant's basketball career affect his children?
4. Was basketball the only sport Kobe ever played?
5. Why did Joe stop playing basketball?

Even though Joe wasn't playing, he wanted to share his knowledge with others. He had helped Kobe become a better players and thought he could do the same for others. So the Bryants moved to Philadelphia in 1992, and Joe took a job as a coach for a women's *varsity* team in Pennsylvania. Kobe remained in Philadelphia until he finished high school.

Much of Kobe's basketball success is due to his father's help over the years. Joe Bryant found a real talent in coaching others to do well on the court. He continued to coach other teams for many years. Eventually, Joe took over as head coach of the Los Angeles Sparks, a team in the Women's National Basketbal Association (WNBA). Some might think Kobe inherited his talent for basketball from his father. But Kobe learned it takes more than that to be a great player. Joe taught Kobe that being a great basketball player takes hard work and determination.

Words to Understand

freshman: First year in high school or college.
drafted: Chosen to play on an NBA team.
rebounds: Getting the ball back after missed shots.
assists: Passes from one player to another that lead to the second player scoring.
playoffs: Games at the end of the season between the top teams in the NBA. The winners of the playoffs face each other for the championship.
lottery: The way teams choose an order for drafting new players. Each NBA team enters the lottery and the team picked first gets its first choice in the draft.

PREPARING FOR THE NBA

Kobe's basketball skills were recognized from the moment he entered high school. He tried out and was picked for the Lower Merion High School's varsity basketball team. Varsity teams are very selective, which means they only take the best players who try out. First-year students don't usually make the varsity team, because they are young and inexperienced. But Kobe was an exception. He was so talented and skilled that he was picked for the varsity team in his *freshman* year. He was the first freshman to make the varsity team in decades.

Kobe was a good player, but he was not a superstar yet. Practicing at home and at school would not be enough to make Kobe great. He needed to find other ways to get better. Kobe found people at a Temple University gym to work out with and play basketball with. One of them was Eddie Jones. At the time, Eddie was playing for the Temple University basketball team. Eddie and Kobe became fast friends and liked to practice together. Kobe looked up to Eddie, because he was one step ahead of Kobe in the basketball world. Eddie was already in college and playing for a university team. Kobe was

The famous Palestra, the home court of the Temple University basketball team. Kobe met Eddie Jones working out at Temple. Eddie went on to join the Lakers before Kobe also joined the LA team.

In basketball, some positions focus on scoring points. They are called the offense. Other positions try to stop the other team from scoring. They are the defense. Kobe played five positions while he was in high school. This made him very versatile. A versatile player has many skills and can fill different roles on a basketball team, depending on what the team needs. Kobe was a very valuable player, because he was able to play any position on the court. In the NBA, Kobe is a guard or small forward.

still in high school. In 1994 Eddie was **drafted** onto Kobe's favorite NBA team, the Los Angeles Lakers.

Kobe's basketball skills improved every year. His third season playing for the Lower Merion Aces was when he really began to shine. By the time Kobe was a junior, he had improved a lot. He averaged an impressive 31 points, 10 **rebounds**, and 5 **assists** per game! It was an outstanding year. His achievements were so great that he was named Pennsylvania Player of the Year. It was Kobe's breakout year, because people all over the country began to notice just how good he was.

In the summer before Kobe's senior year of high school, he began working out with the Philadelphia 76ers. It was the same team Kobe's father played for before he left the NBA. The team was filled with talented players, so Kobe had a chance to practice with some of basketball's best.

When Kobe began his senior year, he was six and a half feet tall and ready to lead the Aces to victory. The Aces won thirty-two games and only lost three that year. The team also won the state title, something Lower Merion High School had not done in over forty years.

Kobe Bryant earned many awards during his senior year of high school. *USA Today* and *Parade* magazine named him National High School Player of the Year. Some companies also recognized his success. He was named to the McDonald's All-American Team and became the Gatorade Circle of Champions High School Player of the Year. By the time Kobe was ready to graduate high school, his popularity was really starting to soar.

THE COLLEGE CHOICE

When Kobe's high school career ended, he had scored a total of 2,883 points. This was the most points ever scored by a Pennsylvania high school basketball player. It was clear he had a bright future ahead of him.

Long before the stadiums filled with fans, Kobe had to decide whether or not to go to college. In the end, Kobe's dream of playing in the NBA didn't depend on college, but for many players, playing for a college team is the only way to make it to the NBA.

Now he had to choose what he would do after high school. Kobe could go to college and play for a college team. Or he could go after his dream of an NBA career immediately. Both options had their pros and cons.

Many colleges tried to recruit Kobe during his junior year of high school. They wanted Kobe to attend their schools after he graduated. Joining a college team had a lot of benefits. If he played basketball in college, he would receive a sports scholarship. Students who receive scholarships can go to school for less money or even for free! If Kobe went to college, he would get a great education and get to play the sport he loved. On the downside, he would have to wait a few more years before trying to join the NBA.

As a senior, Kobe seriously thought about going to college. He had great grades in school and earned a high score on his SAT. The SAT is a standardized test high school students take if they are planning to go to college. The scores from this test are sent to all colleges the student wants to attend as part of his college applications. In this way, the SAT is sort of like an entrance exam. In order to get into a great school, a student needs a very high score. Kobe scored a 1080 out of 1600. His score was more than enough for a sports scholarship to a very good college.

Kobe thought about playing for a number of universities. Some of his top choices were Duke, North Carolina, Villanova, and Michigan. Of these, Kobe has said he probably would have played for Duke if he went to college. In the end, Kobe decided not to go to college. He had been waiting to join the NBA all his life, and he finally had the chance. Kobe didn't want to spend years in college before entering the NBA. Many experts agreed Kobe didn't need to go to college to improve his skills before turning professional. He was ready to join the NBA.

THE NBA DRAFT

The NBA draft is a yearly event where players entering the NBA are chosen to join NBA teams. Players who enter the NBA draft do not get to choose which team they want to play for. If all of the best players entering the draft joined the team with the best record, it wouldn't be fair to the other teams.

Kobe's face is used to sell cars in China. Years after first entering the NBA and signing his first endorsement deals, Kobe is still a huge star. Today, he's still working with companies to sell everything from sneakers to soda.

Making Connections

Most players who decide to enter the NBA draft come from U.S. colleges. If a player has played all the years he can in college (usually four years) and wants a chance to play in the NBA, he can enter the draft. If players haven't finished their college basketball careers, they can still decide to enter the draft. But if they do, they give up the chance to play college basketball. High school players like Kobe could be selected for the NBA right out of high school until the 2006 draft. Now potential NBA players must be at least nineteen years old by the end of the draft year. And they must wait a year after graduation to enter the draft.

The NBA draft process is designed to make it fair for every team involved. Before the draft, representatives of teams that didn't make the **playoffs** meet to take part in a **lottery**. There they learn the order of player selection for the first round of the draft.

During the NBA draft, teams are allowed to make trade agreements. For example, a team might offer to trade one team member for a player from another team. When Kobe entered the draft in 1996, the Charlotte Hornets and the Los Angeles Lakers had decided to make a trade. If the Hornets picked Kobe, the Lakers would give the Hornets another player as part of the deal. The Hornets picked Kobe Bryant thirteenth in the draft. The two teams then made the trade, and Kobe became a Los Angeles Laker.

When Kobe entered the draft, he was just seventeen years old. He wasn't even old enough to sign a contract that would change his life forever. His parents had to sign it for him. The three-year contract gave him more than three million dollars! When Kobe took

Make Connections

Athletes sometimes endorse products. An endorsement is an agreement between a company and an athlete. A company pays the athlete to make its brand look good. For example, when Kobe was signed by Adidas in 1996, he had to wear Adidas shoes. Kobe even had a shoe named after him. There is no limit to the amount of endorsements an athlete may have. Kobe has been endorsed by Coca-Cola, McDonald's, and Nike.

Laker fans fill the Staples Center in Los Angeles, the team's home stadium. Playing for the Lakers changed Kobe's life, giving him a chance to play for a team that's been home to stars like Magic Johnson and Shaquille O'Neal.

the court for his first professional game, he became the youngest person to ever play in an NBA game. He was eighteen years and seventy-two days old at the time. He was living his dream.

Joining the Lakers was the best possible outcome Kobe could have hoped for. It was his favorite team growing up. And Magic Johnson had played for them. But Kobe wasn't just a Laker fan. He had played with them a few times before the NBA draft. The manager of the Lakers had seen Kobe practicing and immediately noticed he was something special.

By joining the Lakers, Kobe was also reunited with his old friend Eddie Jones. They had played together when Kobe was still in high school. Now they would play together on a professional team. Another teammate who joined the Lakers that year was Shaquille O'Neal. He was older and far more experienced than Kobe. With such talented teammates, the Lakers were sure to go far.

Magic Johnson is one of the best basketball players in the history of the sport. During his time with the Lakers, Johnson became one of the NBA's most popular players, alongside legends like Larry Bird and a young Michael Jordan.

Joining the Lakers was a great chance for Kobe to finally show his skills to the world, but, in the end, his first season with the team wouldn't go the way he planned.

Research Projects

In the 1996 draft, the Hornets traded Kobe away to the Lakers. Use the Internet to find out what player they traded Kobe for. Next, find some other examples of trades that were made for rookies that were just drafted. Why would a team like the Hornets agree to trade away a promising young player like Kobe? Look up the record for the player he was traded for. Do you think the Hornets got a good deal?

Text-Dependent Questions

1. Why did Kobe decide not to go to college, even though he was such a strong student?
2. How does the draft system work? How is it designed to make it fair for teams who might not be doing as well?
3. Who is one of the NBA players who inspired Kobe?
4. Who were some of Kobe's teammates when he joined the Lakers?
5. What's the difference between a point guard and a shooting guard?

The first position Kobe played in the NBA was as a guard. Guards need to shoot from a great distance. It is a difficult position to play, because need great aim. Not many players drafted into the NBA start off as guards straight out of high school. There are two different types of guards in the NBA: a point guard and a shooting guard. Point guards handle the ball more, while shooting guards takes shots at the basket from the farthest distance. Kobe is now a shooting guard.

Even as a rising star, Kobe did not know how successful he would become. He has earned a place on many NBA "best" lists. In an interview with ESPN, Kobe was asked how he would have reacted if someone had told his teenage self he would have such a successful career. He said, "If you would have told me back then, I'd say you were nuts. Just nuts. It's hard to believe."

Words to Understand

rookie: First or new, usually used in sports.

former: Refers to someone who used to hold a position but does so no longer.

Making a Mark

Life as a professional basketball player is not easy. Getting used to it can be hard for a new player. When a player is drafted, he must move to the area where his new team plays. Professional basketball players practice many hours each day. If they aren't practicing, they work out to strengthen the muscles they need to play well. Basketball players also travel a lot to compete against other teams.

Like other new NBA players Kobe had to adjust to the lifestyle of a professional athlete. But unlike other new players, Kobe did not have a hard time getting used to his new schedule. He grew up around basketball and saw what his father went through as a professional basketball player. Kobe's lifelong dream was to join the NBA, and by the time he was finally able to do it, he was prepared. Being away from family and friends can be stressful to a new player, but it did not bother Kobe. He was used to traveling, because he did it so much of it as a child.

During his *rookie* year, Kobe did not get to play very often. Rookies are less experienced and usually do not play as well as their older teammates. Some athletes might be

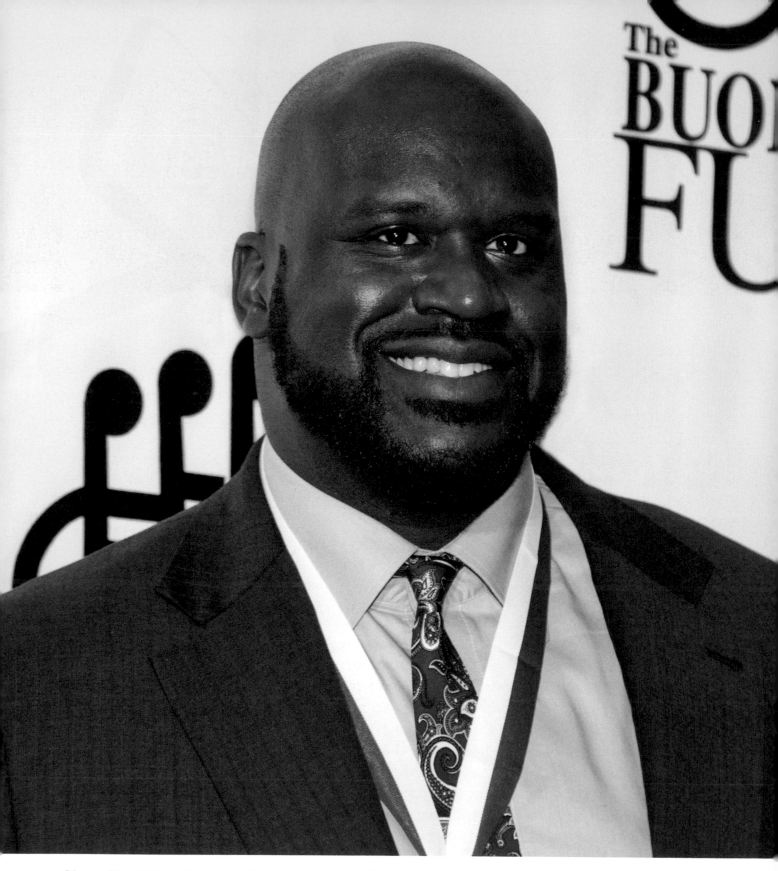

Shaquille O'Neal is one of the most famous Lakers of all time. The NBA legend played for LA for a few years alongside Kobe. Together, the two helped the team win a championship in the 1999-2000 season.

Playing basketball can be tough. Playing a sport all day can wear down an athlete's body and mind. Some days are easier than others. Being able to push through the more difficult days is important. An athlete can't just give up when the going gets tough. If Kobe didn't keep trying to improve, he wouldn't be where he is today. One of his most famous quotes is, "Everything negative—pressures, challenges— is all an opportunity for me to rise." This is great advice for any young athlete. In order to be successful, you have to see every difficult situation as a challenge to be overcome.

unhappy about not getting to play much during their first season, but not Kobe. He just wanted the Lakers to do well. "I'll do whatever it takes to win games, whether it's sitting on a bench waving a towel, handing a cup of water to a teammate, or hitting the game-winning shot," Kobe said.

Kobe saw his rookie year as a chance to prove himself. And he wasted no time showing the world what he was made of. His time on the court increased with each game. Kobe scored at total of 31 points in the All-Star Rookie game. At just eighteen years old, Kobe became the youngest and only Laker to win the Slam Dunk Contest at the All-Star Game, a competition that includes the best players in the NBA. By the end of Kobe's first year, he averaged about fifteen minutes per game. Kobe was a strong player, and his coach definitely noticed it during Kobe's rookie year.

RISING TO THE TOP

In his second year, Kobe continued to improve. He more than doubled his average points per game from 7 to 15 in just one season. Fans from around the world began to notice Kobe's talent and skill. That year, he was voted the youngest NBA All-Star starter in history. Fans vote on who they want to be a part of these games. That year, four players from the Lakers were chosen: Shaquille O'Neal, Nick Van Exel, Eddie Jones, and, of course, Kobe Bryant. Kobe was selected to the NBA All-Star team for a second time in 2000. Since then, he has been chosen for the All-Star team every year through 2013.

By Kobe's third season, the Lakers knew he was a player worth keeping. His contract was extended, and his salary was increased. Professional athletes can make millions each year by playing sports and even more with endorsements. As an athlete gets better, his salary will also improve.

In the 1999–2000 season, the Lakers showed they had what it took to rise to the top. The team had a new coach, Phil Jackson. He was the **former** coach of the Chicago Bulls.

Playing for the Lakers, Kobe has reached amazing heights. The team has had some great players over the years, and now Kobe is one of these Laker legends.

With Phil's help, the Lakers were able to make it to the NBA finals. The team then won its first NBA championship since 1988, when Magic Johnson was still a part of the team. The Lakers continued to conquer the NBA finals for two more years. In 2002 Kobe became the youngest player to win three championships. He was also named the MVP of the NBA All-Star Game.

In the meantime, Kobe's skills just kept getting better. He had been a part of the Lakers for three years by the time he won his first championship. In the 2001–2002 season, Kobe scored about 28 points per game. His average increased to 30 points the next season.

But in 2003, Kobe did not do quite as well. His points per game dropped, and the Lakers did not win the finals. The winning streak stopped at three. Every athlete has good years and bad years. For Kobe, 2003 happened to be a bad one. Shaquille O'Neal, one of the team's best players, joined a new team the following year. This left Kobe and his teammates to work harder for victory.

LEADING THE TEAM

In 2005 Kobe really began to shine as a player and a leader. He averaged 35 points per game, which was the highest of any season he played in the NBA. It was not uncommon for Kobe to score more than 40 points per game. Though 40 points is a lot for one player, it was not good enough for Kobe. He was determined to be the best.

Kobe took his place as one of the best players in NBA history during 2006. In a game against the Toronto Raptors, he scored 81 points. Kobe was the second person in NBA history to do this. The only person to score more points in a game is Wilt Chamberlain, who did it over forty years earlier.

From 2005 to 2007, Kobe had the highest average points per game of any player in the league. During one month, he scored at least 45 points per game for four straight games. At the end of 2007, Kobe reached an important milestone. He scored his 20,000th point, and he was just twenty-nine years old.

All of Kobe's hard work paid off in 2008, when he was named the NBA's Most Valuable Player (MVP). This is an incredible honor, because only one player can be named the MVP each year. There are many talented basketball players in the country, but Kobe was chosen over them all. When Kobe won the award, he said, "It's been a long ride. I'm very proud to represent this organization, to represent this city." It had taken him twelve years

Kobe holds up the championship trophy during the Laker's victory parade in 2009.

KOBE BRYANT

Lakers fans crowd the team's bus during the 2009 championship parade. Kobe is one of basketball's biggest stars and the Lakers are one of the NBA's biggest teams.

to get to this point, and Kobe was far from finished. He wanted to keep playing the sport he loved and break more records while doing it.

The next year was important to Kobe and his teammates. They hadn't won a championship in six seasons and were determined to become champions again. The Lakers easily reached the NBA finals and won. With over 32 points per game, Kobe was named the MVP of the NBA championships. This was his first time to receive the award, but it wouldn't be his last.

Make Connections

Basketball games can be stressful. With the clock counting down, every point matters. Missing just one basket can mean the difference between victory and defeat. Kobe Bryant knows this better than anyone. One of the reasons Kobe is famous is because of his ability to make really tough shots when he needs to. An example of a really hard shot is called a three-pointer. It is worth three points and must be made from past the designated line on the court floor. The person making the shot needs to have perfect aim, because the three-point line is over twenty feet away from the basket! Kobe is known as a clutch player, because he can make these hard shots.

Kobe celebrates with fans at the Lakers Parade in Los Angeles in 2010.

In the 2009–2010 season, Kobe reached another important point in his career. He became the youngest NBA player to ever score 25,000 total points. The Lakers won the NBA championship again that year, making Kobe a five-time champion. He was also named MVP of the championship for a second time in a row. That season Kobe became the all-time leading scorer in Laker history. He had scored more points than even Magic Johnson!

Research Projects

As one of the best basketball players in the world, Kobe has been named the NBA's MVP multiple times. Go online and find out what years he was named the MVP. How many times has he gotten the award? Who are some of the other players who have been named MVP? How do their records stack up against Kobe's?

Text-Dependent Questions

1. Why don't rookies usually get to play as much in games as more experienced players do?
2. What is the NBA All-Star Game? Why is it exciting that Kobe was chosen for it?
3. What is the NBA MVP? How many can there be every year?
4. What is a triple-double? Why is it impressive?

Kobe Bryant is most famous for his ability to score a lot of points in a game, being a well-rounded player is important, too. A good basketball player knows how to assist his teammates, block opponents, and pass the ball to someone who has a good chance to score. In 2009 Kobe proved how well rounded he was when he had a great game and recorded a triple-double. A triple-double is when a basketball player scores double-digits in at least three categories of basketball. For example, a triple-double can be made up of 23 points, 10 assists, and 11 steals. Getting a triple-double is rare. Even the best basketball players only achieve a few each season. As one of the best basketball players in the NBA, Kobe has scored many triple-doubles throughout his career.

In April 2010, Kobe had a choice. He could stay with the Lakers or join another team. His fans wanted him to stay with the Lakers because of the success he brought to the team and to the city of Los Angeles. The Lakers offered him more money to stay. In the end, Kobe decided to resign with the Lakers. This new deal increased his pay to over twenty-four million dollars per year. That's about eight times what he earned as a rookie!

Words to Understand

Achilles tendon: The stretchy cord that attaches your calf muscles to your heel bone. You use it when you walk, run, and jump.

foundation: An organization that works to do good in the world.

STAYING STRONG

Kobe is famous in the United States, but he is also a worldwide champion. His first international gold medal came from the FIBA American Championship. In 2008 Kobe played in the Olympics for the first time. The U.S. team easily took home the gold. Four years later, Kobe played in the Olympics a second time, and his team won again.

Since the Lakers' NBA championship in 2010, Kobe has been unable to snag another title. The Lakers haven't even been able to make it to the NBA finals. Part of the reason the team hasn't done well is because of injuries. Professional athletes get hurt all the time. Sometimes the injury happens because a player pushes himself too hard. For example, Kobe tore his **Achilles tendon** in 2013, when he played for longer than he should have.

When Kobe gets hurt, he does his best to return to the court as quickly as he can. Sometimes this just isn't possible. If an injury is serious enough, an athlete must let it heal before playing again. And it can be hard for the team to do well if many of its regular players are injured. Basketball is a team sport, and every teammate relies on each other to do well.

After winning championships and becoming one of the NBA's biggest stars, Kobe is still working hard to be the best player he can be. He's never stopped trying to improve, no matter how famous or successful he is.

Coach Phil Jackson retired in 2011, which may be another reason the Lakers haven't been doing as well. Learning to work with a new coach can be hard, especially when the last one led the team to five championships. Mike Brown replaced Phil, but he was fired after just one year. Mike D'Antoni became the new head coach in 2013. Before joining the Lakers, he coached many teams, including the New York Knicks.

Even though the Lakers were not doing as well as before, Kobe kept improving his game. He began the 2010–2011 season by breaking even more records. First, he became the youngest player in NBA history to ever score 26,000 points. Then he scored 27,000 points in the same year. His totals keep increasing with every game he plays.

Kobe speaks in front of fans in 2009.

HELPING THE WORLD

As a professional athlete, Kobe wants to give back to the community. One of the ways he does this is through the Kobe & Vanessa Bryant Family Foundation. The foundation began in 2007. It aims to help students get the education they need to be successful in life. It sometimes gives scholarships to the Kobe Bryant Basketball Academy.

Another way Kobe gives back is by teaching others. During the off-season, Kobe spends his time visiting schools throughout the country. He is a part of the After-School All-Stars program, which teaches children about the importance of staying in school and never giving up.

Kobe with his family in 2007. Kobe met his wife Vanessa in the late 1990s, and they have been together ever since. Kobe's family is very important to him.

It is not uncommon for a professional basketball player to switch teams after his or her contract is up. One example is Shaquille O'Neal. Throughout his long career, he played for six NBA teams. Kobe, on the other hand, chooses to stay with the Los Angeles Lakers. It was his favorite team growing up and being a part of it had been a lifelong dream. He is very loyal to the Lakers and does not plan to leave anytime soon.

As a basketball player, Kobe knows sports are an important part of every child's education. That is why he hosts the Kobe Bryant Basketball Academy every year. At the summer camp, children can learn how to be great basketball players, just like Kobe! The camp is a few days long, and Kobe always makes an appearance to give demonstrations and play with the kids. Sometimes he gives speeches about what it takes to become a pro. Each year, children from all over the United States come to California to attend this special camp.

Another way Kobe gives back is by volunteering for the Make-A-Wish Foundation. This foundation grants the wishes of children who are very sick. A wish can be anything from meeting a celebrity to taking a trip to Disney World. People who volunteer for the Make-A-Wish Foundation do everything they can to make a child's wish come true. Since joining, Kobe has granted over a hundred wishes for children all over the United States. For many children, just meeting Kobe is a dream come true.

Famous athletes can do more than just give money or start a **foundation**. They can use their popularity to make a difference, too. People pay attention to celebrities, and Kobe knows this. When a natural disaster strikes anywhere in the world, Kobe jumps into action. He has recorded videos to urge people to donate their money or time to a cause. He even donated a lot of his own money, as well. After Hurricane Katrina, Kobe invited some boys from the devastated area to visit Los Angeles and get a tour of the city.

PERSONAL LIFE

In 1999 Kobe was working on a music project. At the same time, Vanessa Laine was in the building, working as a dancer for a music video. The two met and instantly fell in love. Vanessa was only seventeen at the time and still in high school. Kobe was twenty-one and already playing in the NBA.

Their lives were very different, but Kobe and Vanessa were determined to make it work. They were engaged in May of 2000, just six months after they started dating. Their

Kobe Bryant with basketball legends Magic Johnson (left) and Kareem Abdul-Jabbar (right).

KOBE BRYANT

Make Connections

Some athletes have special nicknames. For basketball players, a nickname usually comes from how a basketball player performs on the court. Kobe's most popular nickname is "Black Mamba." He gets the name from a deadly type of snake. A black mamba is a venomous snake that can strike very fast and has great aim. It is a good nickname for Kobe, because he is quick on his feet and can shoot baskets from a great distance with amazing accuracy. A new nickname Kobe has given himself is "Vino." It is the Italian word for wine. He gave himself this name because he believes his playing style is like wine; it just keeps getting better with age.

wedding took place a year later. Kobe's parents and sisters did not agree with the marriage, because they thought Kobe was too young to be married. They also did not like that Vanessa was not African American.

Everyone in Kobe's immediate family refused to go to his wedding. As a result, Kobe did not talk to his parents for many years. They finally made up when Kobe's first daughter, Natalia Diamante Bryant, was born in 2003. Three years later, their second daughter was born. She is named Gianna Maria-Onore Bryant.

In 2011 Kobe and Vanessa had marriage problems. They wanted to get a divorce, but decided not to. In 2013, the couple decided to work to make their marriage stronger.

Kobe makes millions of dollars playing for the Los Angeles Lakers. He can afford many expensive things, including the large mansion he bought for himself and his family. They live in Newport Beach, which is about an hour away from Los Angeles, so Kobe doesn't have to drive very far to get to practice each day.

Kobe doesn't use the Internet very often. In fact, one of the few times he uses Google is

Text-Dependent Questions

1. Why hasn't Kobe been able to get another title since 2010?
2. What is the Kobe and Vanessa Bryant Family Foundation? When was it founded?
3. What is the Make-A-Wish Foundation? How does Kobe help out with it?
4. Why didn't Kobe's family want to go to his wedding?
5. How many times have Kobe been named an NBA All-Star?

to help his daughters with their homework! He does have his own website, though. It can be found at kobebryant.com. Kobe is also on Twitter and has over three million followers. Fans can follow his page to keep up with his life both on and off the court. The Twitter page can be found at twitter.com/kobebryant.

Kobe Bryant has a lot to be proud of. He has been named an NBA All-Star fifteen times and helped the Lakers win five championships. Kobe followed in his father's footsteps to become one of the greatest players of all time. Magic Johnson, a former Laker, has even said some great things about Kobe. According to Magic, Kobe is, "the closest thing to Michael Jordan that I have ever seen." He has also called Kobe, "the greatest Laker ever." When asked how he felt about Magic saying that, Kobe responded, "Words can't describe it. He was my favorite player growing up, and coming from him it couldn't have meant more." Magic's words were proof that Kobe had become one of the basketball legends he loved to watch growing up. Today, Kobe inspires young people around the world to believe they can become the next NBA star just like him.

Series Glossary of Key Terms

All-Star Game: A game where the best players in the league form two teams and play each other.

Assist: A pass that leads to scoring points. The player who passes the ball before the other scores a basket gets the assist.

Center: A player, normally the tallest on the team, who tries to score close to the basket and defend against the other team's offense using his size.

Championship: A set of games between the two top teams in the NBA to see who is the best.

Court: The wooden or concrete surface where basketball is played. In the NBA, courts are 94 feet by 50 feet.

Defensive: Working to keep the other team from scoring points.

Draft (noun): The way NBA teams pick players from college or high school teams.

Foul: A move against another player that is against the rules, mostly involving a player touching another in a way that is not fair play.

Jump shot: A shot made from far from the basket (rather than under the basket) while the player is in the air.

Offensive: Working to score points against the other team.

Playoffs: Games at the end of the NBA season between the top teams in the league, ending in the finals, in which the two top teams play each other.

Point guard: The player leading the team's offense, scoring points and setting up other players to score.

Power forward: A player who can both get in close to the basket and shoot from further away. On defense, power forwards defend against both close and far shots.

Rebound: Getting the ball back after a missed shot.

Rookie: A player in his first year in the NBA.

Scouts: People who search for new basketball players in high school or college who might one day play in the NBA.

Shooting guard: A player whose job is to take shots from far away from the basket. The shooting guard is usually the team's best long-range shooter.

Small forwards: Players whose main job is to score points close to the basket, working with the other players on the team's offense.

Steal: Take the ball from a player on the other team.

Tournament: A series of games between different teams in which the winning teams move on to play other winning teams and losing teams drop out of the competition.

Find Out More

ONLINE

Kobe Bryant Stats, News, Videos, Highlights, Pictures, Bio
espn.go.com/nba/player/_/id/110

Kobe Bryant (kobebryant) on Twitter
twitter.com/kobebryant

Official Website of Kobe Bryant
kobebryant.com

Kobe Bryant Stats, Video, Bio, Profile | NBA.com
www.nba.com/playerfile/kobe_bryant

IN BOOKS

Gitlin, Marty. *Kobe Bryant: NBA Champion (Playmakers)*. New York: Abdo Publishing Company, 2011.

Osier, Dan. *Kobe Bryant (Basketball's MVPs)*. New York: Powerkids, 2011.

Savage, Jeff. *Kobe Bryant (Amazing Athletes)*. Minneapolis, Minn.: Lerner Publishing Group, 2010.

Thornley, Stew. *Kobe Bryant: Champion Basketball Star (Sports Star Champions)*. Berkeley Heights, N.J.: Enslow Publishing, 2012.

Torsiello, David P. *Read About Kobe Bryant (I Like Sports Stars!)*. Berkeley Heights, N.J.: Enslow Elementary, 2011.

Index

About the Author

Shaina Indovino is a writer and illustrator living in Nesconset, New York. She graduated from Binghamton University, where she received degrees in sociology and English.

Picture Credits